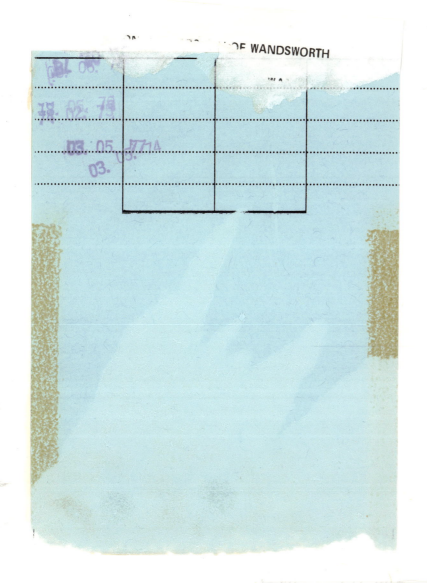

INFANTRY, MOUNTAIN AND AIRBORNE GUNS

WORLD WAR 2 FACT FILES

Infantry, Mountain and Airborne Guns

PETER CHAMBERLAIN AND TERRY GANDER

MACDONALD AND JANE'S
LONDON

940. 531 862 341 CHAM

Q 940. 541

m62495

623.41 CHAM

10009 2388

First published in Great Britain in 1975 by
Macdonald and Jane's (Macdonald & Co. (Publishers) Ltd.)
Paulton House, 8 Shepherdess Walk, London N1 7LW

Printed by Tinling (1973) Limited, Prescot, Merseyside
(a member of the Oxley Printing Group Ltd.)

ISBN 0 356 08225 3

Introduction

This Fact File could well have been sub-titled Lightweight Artillery for it deals with the specialised artillery used for roles which require it to be used under particularly difficult conditions where mobility and light weight have to be combined. The most obvious of these roles at the beginning of World War Two was the mountain gun but another and newer type of specialised artillery piece was the infantry gun. During the course of World War Two another type of specialised weapon that gradually came into prominence was the airborne gun which at first was merely a revised mountain or infantry weapon, but by 1945 many weapons that had been specially designed for this exacting role were in service.

The infantry gun in use in 1939 had been developed to meet a need that had its origins in the trench conflict of World War One. Western Front fighting often depended on massed artillery fire for its major striking power but such fire was difficult and cumbersome to control. Thus the infantryman in his front line trench often felt the need for a more personal form of fire support. By 1916 this personal fire support had evolved into the rudimentary trench mortar and the introduction of light portable guns designed for use in the front line by the infantryman. Typical of this group of guns was the little French 37 mm mle 1916 which was still in use in 1939. It was light, simple and portable and it gave the hard-pressed front line soldier a measure of fire support where and when he needed it most. After 1918 the armies of Europe issued specifications for infantry guns, but not many were in use in 1939. One reason for this was that in most countries the finance for new weapons was not forthcoming, and in others the light mortar was seen as a viable alternative which was simpler and cheaper. The United Kingdom was one example of this trend for in 1932 it was intended to replace the proposed 3.7-inch howitzer with the 3-inch mortar. In Germany, however, it was decided to go ahead with purpose-built infantry guns and the results were the 7.5 cm leIG 18 and the large 15 cm sIG 33. The German infantry battalion made special provision for the manpower needed to serve these weapons so they continued to use infantry guns in large numbers until 1945. Such was their need for infantry guns that the arsenals of occupied countries were plundered for suitable weapons and large numbers were taken into service. One of the largest suppliers was the USSR for they also were advocates of the infantry possessing their own fire support. Japan produced a remarkable little 70 mm gun that was probably one of the best guns ever made for infantry support. This was the Type 92 battalion gun which was encountered all over the Far East theatre. The Italians did give their infantry their own guns but these were usually mountain guns which had been passed over to the infantry when their best days had gone by. Many other states followed this example, and thus many Skoda guns were used by infantry units. Both the USA and the United Kingdom placed their reliance in the mortar for infantry support. This lead was followed by the Commonwealth and colonies, but a 95 mm design for an infantry gun was produced in the United Kingdom in 1943. It underwent troop trials but was not accepted for service.

The first mountain guns appeared in Europe around the turn of the century. They were usually light in calibre and weight and could be broken down into sub-assemblies for pack transport by animals or even men. Another feature was their small physical size for use in confined spaces, and their extreme robustness which led to many of the guns designed before the First War being still in use during the Second. One firm stood out above all others in the design and manufacture of these guns and that was the Czech firm of Skoda who produced the M.15 which was probable the most widely used of all mountain guns. Many of the pieces the Skoda firm produced in the heavier 100 and 105 mm calibres were large and heavy and were virtually field guns with special features for mountain warfare. For the purposes of this File we have decided to include those guns that were given mountain designations by their users or by the manufacturer, and the field guns will be covered in the appropriate Fact File. By 1939 Italy and Germany had produced new designs of mountain guns as had Skoda and Japan, but many of the older guns soldiered on. The Germans never had enough guns to fully equip their mountain units with German designs so many captured guns were impressed into the German mountain gun armoury.

1940 saw the use of airborne troops in action for the first time and as the war progressed the use of airborne troops increased both in numbers and scale until airborne units grew to such a size that they demanded their own artillery support arm. At first, existing infantry and mountain guns were used, but new and more specialised designs were produced. The best example of this pattern was the equipment of the German Fallschirmjäger. Their first artillery equipment was a modified 7.5 cm

1

leIG 18 or a strengthened 10.5 cm GebH 40. But to provide the combination of light weight, strength, mobility and hitting power that the delivery of a useful artillery piece into action the airborne role demands, the Germans produced the recoilless gun. In the recoilless gun the recoil mechanism can be dispensed with because recoil forces are cancelled out by the mass of the propellant gases escaping through a breech venturii. The result is a very light gun that can fire a conventionally-sized shell, and the Germans produced versions in both 75 and 105 mm with even larger calibres on the drawing board. The recoilless gun worked well but the Germans soon discovered that they had severe tactical limitations. The escape of the exhaust gases to the rear of a recoilless gun produced not only a lethal fire hazard but also stirred up large clouds of dust and debris which made concealment difficult. Another drawback to the principle was that the recoilless gun demands a greater ratio of propellant to projectile when compared with the conventional gun, and by 1945 the Germans were turning away from the recoilless gun as their raw material situation became steadily more difficult. Such supply limitations did not apply in the USA where the 57 and 75 mm Kromuskit rifles were produced for service. In many ways the recoilless gun provides the best answer to the problem of equipping the infantry, mountain and airborne artillery arms and in 1974 the recoilless gun is in service throughout the world in many roles, but the problem of the backblast has never been overcome even though the propellant problem has been largely solved.

To return to 1939 to 1945, the recoilless gun did not enter service in sufficient numbers to replace the conventional and often ageing pieces in service in the various lightweight roles. Attempts by the Germans to use the recoilless gun in the infantry and mountain roles met with some success but the numbers involved were small. But they showed the way that lightweight artillery would follow in the future, even if many armies in 1974 still use the American M1A1 or the Japanese Type 92,41 or 94. Also still in use is the Russian 76-43 infantry gun, but the others have nearly all passed away. Thus, World War Two was the last war of the old lightweight artillery and this Fact File provides a record of the ingenuity and skill of the men who designed and used such specialised weapons.

Photo Credits

Imperial War Museum
U.S. Official
Bundesarchiv
E.C. Armees
Ian Hogg
K. R. Pawlas
Bruno Benvenuti
SME Ufficio Storico

AUSTRALIA

Ordnance, Q.F., 25 pr Short Mark 1 (Aust.)

DATA
CALIBRE 87.6 mm   3.45 in
LENGTH OF BARREL WITH CAP   1620.2 mm
  63.788 in
LENGTH OF BARREL W/O CAP   1265.5 mm
  49.825 in
LENGTH OF BORE   1262 mm   49.69 in
WEIGHT COMPLETE   1368.8 kg   3015 lb
ELEVATION   −5° to 40°
TRAVERSE   8°
M.V. (MAX)   390 m/sec   1280 ft/sec
MAXIMUM RANGE   9333 m   10200 yards
SHELL WEIGHT   11.35 kg   25 lb

During 1943 a shortened version of the 25 pr fieldgun-howitzer was produced in Australia and was promptly christened the 'Baby 25 pr'. The basic 25 pr design was drastically revised and bore little resemblance to the original, and the revised carriage became the Carriage 25 pr Light, Mark 1 (Aust.). As the gun was intended for jungle warfare it could be broken down into thirteen loads but a jeep was intended as the towing vehicle when complete and a castor wheel could be fitted under the box trail for manhandling. A muzzle cap was fitted to prevent muzzle flash damaging the recoil cylinder when the barrel recoiled. The short barrel was the design's major shortcoming for range was reduced from the normal 25 pr range of 13,500 yards down to 10,200 yards, and when a version of the 25 pr appeared with a shortened axle (the Carriage, 25 pr, Mark 2) this was preferred to the Baby. However, some Short 25 pr guns did see service in South-East Asia and the Pacific, some in the hands of American troops.

Baby 25 pr in action with American troops in New Guinea

3

BELGIUM

Canon de 75 modele 1934

The standard Belgian mountain gun was the mle 1934 produced by Cockerill. It was produced in relatively small numbers, but was a thoroughly modern design with pneumatic wheels which were rather unusual features on a mountain gun. The box trail could fold for transport but alternatively the gun could be broken down into five loads. After 1940 there are German records of this gun being given the designation of 7.5 cm GebK 228(b) but there is no mention of them using it for any purpose.

DATA
CALIBRE 75 mm 2.95 in
LENGTH OF PIECE (L/24) 1800 mm 70.87 in
LENGTH OF BARREL 1583 mm 62.32 in
LENGTH OF RIFLING 1296.7 mm 51.05 in
WEIGHT IN ACTION 928 kg 2046 lb
ELEVATION (long trail) −10° to 50°
TRAVERSE 8°
M.V. 455 m/s 1493 ft/sec
MAXIMUM RANGE 9300 m 10174 yards
SHELL WEIGHT 6.59 kg 14.53 lb

Canon de 76 FRC

The Belgian infantry support weapon was a 76 mm gun produced by the Fonderie Royale des Canons (FRC). Very little is known about it but it would appear that an alternative 47 mm barrel could be fitted in place of the 76 mm barrel. When travelling long distances the gun was carried on a trailer behind a small tracked vehicle or truck. In 1940 the Germans took over a few as the 7.6 cm IG 260(b). At the start of the war there were 198 in service.

DATA
CALIBRE 76 mm 2.99 in
LENGTH OF PIECE (L/9.2) 699 mm 27.53 in
LENGTH OF BARREL (L/7.8) 593 mm 23.34 in
WEIGHT TRAVELLING 275 kg 606.4 lb
WEIGHT IN ACTION 243 kg 535.8 lb
ELEVATION −6° to 80°
TRAVERSE 40°
M.V. 160 m/s 525 ft/sec
MAXIMUM RANGE 2200m 2407 yards
SHELL WEIGHT 4.64 kg 10.23 lb

Canon de 76 FRC fitted with 47 mm barrel

CZECHOSLOVAKIA

Skoda 75 mm Model 15

DATA
CALIBRE 75 mm 2.95 in
LENGTH OF PIECE (L/15.4) 1155 mm
 45.47 in
LENGTH OF BORE 990 mm 38.97 in
LENGTH OF RIFLING (L/10.7) 802.5 mm
 31.594 in
WEIGHT IN ACTION 613 kg 1351.6 lb
ELEVATION −10° to 50°
TRAVERSE 7°
M.V. (max) 349 m/s 1145 ft/sec
MAXIMUM RANGE 8250 m 9025 yards
SHELL WEIGHT (mod 32) 6.388 kg 14.085
 lb

The Skoda M.15 was one of the most widely used of all the European mountain guns and by many accounts, one of the best. It first entered service with the Austria-Hungarian Army and after 1918 passed into service with the Czech and Austrian armies as well as that of Hungary. Others were obtained by Rumania, Bulgaria and Turkey. Large numbers were captured by Italy who used them as the Obice da 75/13 until the Germans took them over as the 7.5 cm GebK 259(i). The Germans also had large numbers of the M.15 themselves which they had taken over from the Czechs and Austrians. They were meant to be only substitute guns until the GebG 36 entered service but they remained in use until 1945. The German designation was 7.5 cm GebK 15 and guns from Poland and Jugoslavia were added to the German armoury under the same heading. The M.15 dismantled into four loads comprising six sub-assemblies (plus the shield if fitted). Like most mountain guns the design was rugged and straightforward and it gave its many users good service.

5

1

1, 2, 3. *Skoda 75 mm Model 15* **4.** *Skoda Model 15 in service with the Czech Army prior to 1938* **5.** *Obice da 75/13* **6.** *Obice da 75/13 in action in Tunisia during 1943* **7.** *Obice da 75/13*

2

3

4

5

6

7

8

9

10

8. *An Italian mountain unit ready for a move* **9, 12, 13, 14.** *7.5 cm GebK 15*
10. *Mountain gunnery the hard way, with an Italian unit carrying a 75/13*
11. *An Obice da 75/13 with rubber tyres for tractor towing. Note the figure in the mid-background.*

11

12

13

14

Skoda 75 mm and 90 mm Model 1928 (CD/DC)

The Skoda M.28 was produced as an export model for Jugoslavia and was a revised and updated version of the Skoda M.15. One unusual feature of this weapon was that it could take a 90 mm barrel as an alternative to its normal 75 mm fitting. Barrels of both calibres were sold to Jugoslavia but only the 75 mm barrel was used to any extent and contemporary German sources make no mention of any being captured during the fighting there. The Germans gave captured guns the comprehensive and cumbersome title of 7.5 cm GebK 28 (in Einheitslafette mit 9 cm GebH and compounded the situation by also referring to it as the 7.5 cm GebK 285(j) Many of the ex-Jugoslav guns were issued to the pro-German Croat forces. The data refers to the 75 mm version only.

DATA
CALIBRE 75 mm 2.95 in
LENGTH OF PIECE (L/18) 1345 mm 52.95 in
WEIGHT IN ACTION 710 kg 1565.5 lb
ELEVATION −8° to 50°
TRAVERSE 7°
M.V. 425 m/s 1394 ft/sec
MAXIMUM RANGE 8700 mm 9518 yards
SHELL WEIGHT 6.3 kg 13.9 lb

1, 2. *Skoda 75 mm Model 1928*

1

2

Skoda 75 mm Model 1936 (C5)—Russian 76-38

In 1936 Skoda produced a new design of mountain gun in a calibre of 75 mm. Although it roused little interest elsewhere the Russians were very impressed with its potential and licence-built the design as their own 76.2 mm Mountain Gun Model 1938 or 76-38. Skodas did build a few prototypes of the gun in 76.2 mm but the Russians produced the gun in some numbers and after 1938 the gun may be considered as a Russian weapon as no other country obtained any until after 1945. The gun could be broken down into three basic units for towing but could be further broken down into ten loads for pack transport. Any that fell into German hands became the 7.62 mm GebK 307(r) and the Germans found them very sound and useful guns.

DATA
CALIBRE 762 mm 3 in
LENGTH OF PIECE (L/21.4) 1630 mm
  64.17 in
LENGTH OF BARREL (L/18.7) 1430 mm
  56.3 in
LENGTH OF RIFLING 1122.1 mm
  44.177 in
WEIGHT IN ACTION 785 kg 1731 lb
ELEVATION −8° to 65°
TRAVERSE 10°
M.V. 495 m/s 1624 ft/sec
MAXIMUM RANGE 10100 m 11050 yards
SHELL WEIGHT 6.23 kg 13.737 lb

Skoda 75 mm Model 1939(C6)

The appearance of the Skoda M.1939 mountain gun would indicate that its design owed much to that of the Bofors L/22 gun exported to Switzerland. The Skoda gun was produced for export to Rumania and Iran but in relatively small numbers only. It could be dismantled into eight loads for transport by mule and used a shield with a very pronounced angle of slope. In Rumania the guns were used to equip two mountain artillery battalions.

DATA

CALIBRE 75 mm 2.95 in
LENGTH OF PIECE (L/21) 1575 mm 62 in
WEIGHT IN ACTION 820 kg 1808 lb
ELEVATION (maximum possible) −30° to
 70°

TRAVERSE 7°
M.V. 480 m/s 1575 ft/sec
MAXIMUM RANGE 10200 m 11159 yards
SHELL WEIGHT 6.3 kg 13.9 lb

Skoda 100 mm Model 1916

For a mountain artillery piece, the Skoda M.16 was a large and heavy design. It could be broken down into three loads for towing by two-animal carts which rather restricted its use in difficult country but the M.16 was a widely-used weapon. In Germany the M.16 was known as the 10 cm GebH 16 or 16(ö). The Italians designated their guns the Obice da 100/17 modello 16 and any that were left in service after 1943 passed into German use as the 10 cm GebH 316(i). Czech guns were known to the Germans as the 10 cm GebH 16 or 16(t) after 1938. Other nations that used the M.16 were Jugoslavia and Poland, while Turkey used a 105 mm version known as the M.16(T).

DATA

CALIBRE 100 mm 3.9 in
LENGTH OF PIECE (L/19) 1930 mm
 75.98 in
LENGTH OF BARREL 1705 mm 67.125 in
LENGTH OF RIFLING 1500 mm 59 in
WEIGHT TRAVELLING 2150 kg 4741 lb
WEIGHT IN ACTION 1235 kg 2723 lb
ELEVATION −8° to 70°

TRAVER;E 3° right, 2.5° left
M.V. (Czech/Italian) 341/407 m/s
 1119/1335 ft/sec
MAXIMUM RANGE (Czech/Italian) 7750/
 9280 m 7090/8490 yards
SHELL WEIGHT (Czech/Italian) 16/13.37 kg
 35.3/29.48 lb

*Obice da 100/17 modello 16 on tow by a
Fiat 708 OCI light mountain tractor*

11

Obice da 100/17 modello 16

Obice da 100/17 at El Adem, September 1940

Obice da 100/17 in action, probably in Russia

Skoda 100 mm Model 16/19

The M.16/19 was developed from the M.16 and differed mainly in using a longer barrel. In most other respects it was similar to the earlier model. The main users of the M.16/19 prior to 1938 was the Czech Army who used the gun in both 100 mm and 105 mm. After 1938 both types were impressed into German service as the 10 cm GebH 16/19(t) and the 10.5 cm GebH(t). Some guns were sent to Turkey and a few were sent to Italy.

DATA
CALIBRE   100 mm   3.9 in
LENGTH OF PIECE (L/24)   2400 mm   94.5 in
WEIGHT IN ACTION   1350 kg   2977 lb
ELEVATION   −7.5° to 70°
TRAVERSE   5.5°
M.V.   395 m/s   1296 ft/sec
MAXIMUM RANGE   9800 m   10720 yards
SHELL WEIGHT   16 kg   35.3 lb

1, 3, 5. *10.5 cm GebH(t) ready for mountain transport* **2.** *Skoda 100 mm Model 16/19* **4.** *10.5 cm GebH(t)*

1

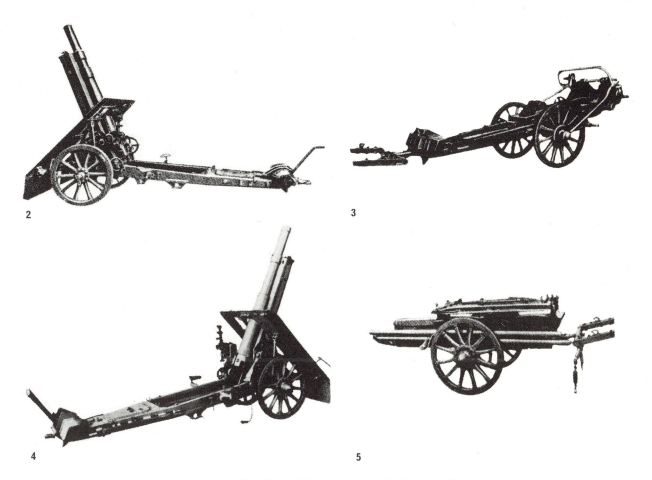

2

3

4

5

Skoda 105 mm Model 1939(D9)

To provide the heavier firepower needed to back up that provided by the 75 mm M.39, the Skoda works produced the 105 mm M.39 howitzer. It was ordered by Rumania. The M.39 was merely a revised version of the weapons produced in the M.16 and M.16/19 family and differed from them in no appreciable way. A very similar howitzer was produced for Afghanistan.

DATA
CALIBRE   105 mm   4134 in
LENGTH OF PIECE (L/23.9)   2510 mm
   98.8 in
WEIGHT IN ACTION   1400 kg   3087 lb
ELEVATION   −7°30′ to 70°

TRAVERSE   6°
M.V.   450 m/s   1476 ft/sec
MAXIMUM RANGE   1100 m   1203 yards
SHELL WEIGHT   15 kg   33 lb

Skoda 150 mm Model 1918

To the Skoda 150 mm M.18 must go the distinction of being the heaviest mountain gun ever produced. It weighed 2800 kg (6174 lb) in action and was a very awkward gun to move around so it is not surprising to learn that it was produced in very small numbers only. The design was produced during World War One and the prototype was ready only as the war ended. Czechoslovakia used the few guns made and after 1938 the type appears in German records as the 15 cm GebH 18(t). When broken down the gun could be carried on six carts, each towed by two horses or mules pulling in tandem. One of these loads, the barrel assembly, needed three towing animals.

DATA
CALIBRE   149 mm   5.866 in
LENGTH OF PIECE (L/13)   1937 mm
   76.26 in
WEIGHT IN ACTION   2800 kg   6174 lb
ELEVATION   −5° to 70°

TRAVERSE   7°
M.V.   340 m/s   1115 ft/sec
MAXIMUM RANGE (approx)   8000 m
   8750 yards
SHELL WEIGHT   42 kg   92.61 lb

FRANCE

Canon d'Infantrie de 37 mle 1916 TRP

The 37 mm mle 1916 was designed to give the front line troops in the World War One trenches some measure of artillery support for both the attack and in defence. It was a light, handy weapon ideally suited for use in trench warfare but after 1918 it remained in service with the French Army as a general infantry support weapon and in 1939 it was still in front-line service. By that time it was really obsolete but as there was little else to replace it, apart from mortars, it remained in use, especially in the colonies. The mle 1916 was a simple weapon consisting of a short barrel on a steel tripod. Small wheels were used for towing but were removed in action. The gun was accurate and could fire a wide range of projectiles, including an unusual message canister. For pack transport the gun could be dismantled into three loads. The Germans took over the few that remained in service after 1940 as the 3.7 cm IG 152(f) and issued them to second- and third-line occupation troops. The Japanese used a very similar gun based on the mle 1916 as the Type 11. During World War One the American Army took over large numbers of the mle 1916 as the 37 mm Gun M1916 but by 1941 those remaining were in storage or had already been scrapped.

DATA

CALIBRE 37 mm 1.456 in
LENGTH OF PIECE (L/22) 814 mm 32 in
WEIGHT IN ACTION 108 kg 238 lb
WEIGHT TRAVELLING 160.5 kg 353.9 lb
ELEVATION −8° to 17°

TRAVERSE 35°
M.V. 367 m/s 1204 ft/sec
MAXIMUM RANGE 2400 m 2625 yards
SHELL WEIGHT 0.555 kg 1.22 lb

Canon de 65 M(montagne) mle 1906

The little mle 1906 was designed by Schneider-Ducrest and entered service in 1906 with the French Army mountain units (regiments d'artillerie de montagne). By 1939 it had almost passed out of service with the mountain troops and had been passed over to the infantry as a support weapon. The mle 1906 was a very light gun that employed the counter-recoil or soft-recoil system in which the gun is released forward to fire and fires when the barrel is in the forward position. Thus many of the recoil forces are taken up in moving the barrel to the rear against its inertia and the recoil system is lighter as a result. This system has been little used elsewhere and is only now, in 1974, being considered again for new weapons. The mle 1906 could be dismantled into four pack loads and a small trail castor wheel was provided for manhandling the gun into position. After 1940 the Germans took over some mle 1906 guns as the 6.5 cm GebK 221(f) and issued them to their own mountain units. Poland bought some mle 1906 guns after 1918 and in 1939 they were still in service. When some Polish troops left their country after the German invasion they took some of these guns with them, and they remained with them when the Poles were used as part of the Palestine garrison in 1940. Greece and Albania were two other states that used the mle 1906.

DATA
CALIBRE 65 mm 2.56 in
LENGTH OF PIECE (L/20.5) 1334 mm 52.52 in
WEIGHT IN ACTION 400 kg 882 lb
ELEVATION −9°30′ to 35°

TRAVERSE 6°
M.V. 330 m/s 1083 ft/sec
MAXIMUM RANGE 6500 m 7111 yards
SHELL WEIGHT 4.4 kg 9.7 lb

15

Canon de 75 M(montagne) mle 1919 Schneider

As early as 1914 the French mountain artillery officers had decided that they needed a heavier gun than the 65 mm mle 1906. They issued a requirement for a 75 mm gun and the mle 1919 was the result. Produced by Schneider, the mle 1919 was too late for service in the First War and lived on to see action in the Second War. It was a sturdy efficient design that could fire existing 75 mm ammunition, and it was designed to break down into seven loads for pack carriage. As well as entering French service, the mle 1919 was sold to Greece, Poland and Jugoslavia. After the events of 1939 and 1940 large numbers of the mle 1919 fell into German hands and the French guns then became the 7.5 cm GebK 237(f). The Jugoslav guns became the 7.5 cm GebK 283(j), and Polish guns became the 7.5 cm GebK M.19(p)—this latter designation is unconfirmed.

DATA

CALIBRE   75 mm   2.95 in
LENGTH OF PIECE (L/18.6)   1398 mm   55.04 in
LENGTH OF RIFLING   1063 mm   41.85 in
WEIGHT TRAVELLING   721 kg   1589.5 lb
WEIGHT IN ACTION   660 kg   1455 lb
ELEVATION   −10° to 40°
TRAVERSE   10°
M.V.   400 m/s   1312 ft/sec
MAXIMUM RANGE   9025 m   9873 yards
SHELL WEIGHT   6.33 kg   13.95 lb

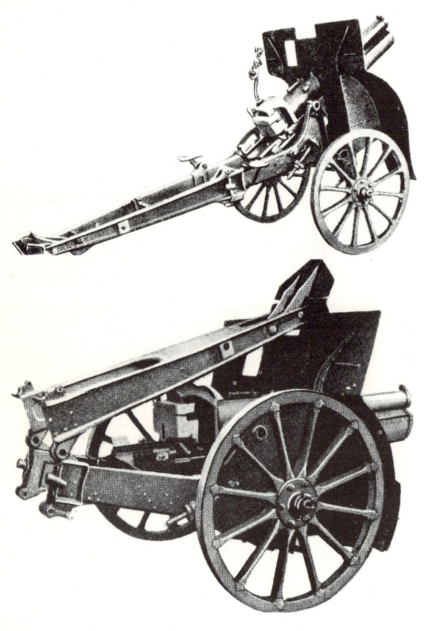

Canon de 75 M(montagne) mle 1928

DATA
CALIBRE   75 mm   2.95 in
LENGTH OF PIECE (L/18.6)   1397 mm
  55 in
LENGTH OF RIFLING   1060 mm   47.73 in
WEIGHT TRAVELLING   721 kg   1589.5 lb
WEIGHT IN ACTION   660 kg   1455 lb
ELEVATION   −10° to 40°
TRAVERSE   10°
M.V.   375 m/s   1230 ft/sec
MAXIMUM RANGE   9000 m   9846 yards
SHELL WEIGHT   7.25 kg   15.98 lb

The design of the Schneider mle 1928 owed little to that of the earlier mle 1919 as it used a different carriage (the trail remained the same) and the barrel fired heavier ammunition. The recoil mechanism was moved to above the barrel and the shield shape was changed to a simpler form. Like the mle 1919, the mle 1928 entered service with the French Army and was also sold to Poland. After 1940 the French guns were impressed into German use as the 7.5 cm GebK 238(f).

Canon de 76 M(montagne) mle 1909 Schneider

In 1906 a Greek, Col. Danglis, designed a mountain gun which was accepted by the Greek Army. The gun was built in 75 mm calibre by the French Schneider firm and the result was the Schneider-Danglis 06/09 gun with a L/16.67 barrel. By 1939 the gun had passed from Greek service and many had been sold to Finland who used them in the Winter War of 1939-1940. In 1909 an export model had been produced in 76.2 mm calibre for Russia. This version was known to the Russians as the Mountain Gun Model 1909 or 76-09. In 1941 the Germans captured sufficient to use them as the 7.62 cm GebK 293(r). The design of the mle 1909 was sturdy but unremarkable although there were numerous small variations in shield and trail design. It could be dismantled into seven loads for transport.

DATA (76-09)

CALIBRE 76.2 mm 3 in
LENGTH OF PIECE (L/16.5) 1258 mm 49.53 in
LENGTH OF RIFLING (L/15.3) 1165 mm 45.86 in
WEIGHT TRAVELLING 1225 kg 2701 lb

WEIGHT IN ACTION 627 kg 1328.5 lb
ELEVATION −6° to 28°
TRAVERSE 50°
M.V. 387 m/s 1270 ft/sec
MAXIMUM RANGE 8550 m 9354 yards
SHELL WEIGHT 6.23 kg 13.74 lb

1. Greek Schneider-Danglis 06/09 75 mm gun 2-6. Russian 76-09

1

2

3

4

5

6

Canon Court de 105 M(montagne) mle 1909 Schneider

To complement the 76.2 mm mle 1909 guns ordered in 1909, the Russians also ordered some 105 mm howitzers at the same time. These howitzers were known to the Russians as the 105 mm Mountain Howitzer 1909S or 105-09. They served on until World War Two when they were also used as infantry guns. Any that fell into German hands were used as the 10.5 cm GebH 343(r).

DATA

CALIBRE   105 mm   4.134 in
LENGTH OF PIECE (L/10.5)   1102 mm   43.4 in
WEIGHT TRAVELLING   750 kg   1654 lb
WEIGHT IN ACTION   730 kg   1610 lb

ELEVATION   0° to 60°
TRAVERSE   5°
M.V.   300 m/s   984 ft/sec
MAXIMUM RANGE   6000 m   6564 yards
SHELL WEIGHT   12 kg   26.46 lb

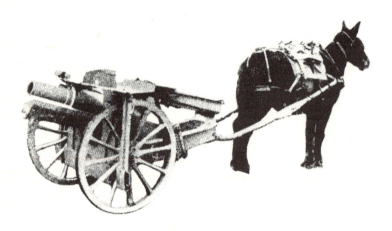

1, 3. Canon Court de 105 M(montagne) mle 1919 Schneider 2. Canon Court de 105 M(montagne) mle 1928

Canon Court de 105 M(montagne) mle 1919 Schneider

The 105 mm mle 1919 was intended to complement the 75 mm mle 1919 and entered service with the French at the same time. It was also exported to Spain and Jugoslavia. This howitzer was designed to break down into eight parts and to ensure that the barrel would not be too heavy for one load it could be dismantled into two loads. In 1939 the French guns were taken over by the Germans as the 10.5 cm le.GebH 322(f) and in 1941 captured Jugoslav guns became the 10.5 cm le.GebH 329(j). In 1928 another model of this gun was produced as the mle 1928 but it differed only in detail from the mle 1919. After 1940 it became the 10.5 cm le.GebH 323(f).

DATA (mle 1919)

CALIBRE   105 mm   4.134 in
LENGTH OF PIECE (L/12.4)   1304 mm   51.34 in
LENGTH OF RIFLING   988 mm   38.9 in
WEIGHT IN ACTION   750 kg   1653.75 lb
ELEVATION   0° to 40°
TRAVERSE   9°
M.V.   350 m/s   1148 ft/sec
MAXIMUM RANGE   7850 m   8588 yards
SHELL WEIGHT   12 kg   26.46 lb

1

2

3

GERMANY

2 cm Gebirgsflak 38

The Gebirgsflak 38 was the 2 cm barrel from the Flak 38 placed on the light carriage of the projected Gerät 239, and it was first produced in 1941. It entered service in 1942 with the German Gebirgstruppen who used it not only as an anti-aircraft gun but also as an anti-tank weapon and for attacking ground targets. As the carriage was really too light for its purpose it was not possible to fire long bursts from the gun as accuracy became very poor.

DATA

CALIBRE 20 mm 0.79 in
LENGTH OF PIECE 2252.5 mm 88.68 in
LENGTH OF RIFLING 720 mm 28.35 in
LENGTH OVERALL 3650 mm 143.7 in
WIDTH 1200 mm 47.25 in
HEIGHT 1270 mm 50 in
WEIGHT COMPLETE 315 kg 695 lb
WEIGHT IN ACTION 276 kg 608.6 lb
ELEVATION −28° to 90°

TRAVERSE 360°
MAXIMUM EFFECTIVE CEILING 2200 m
  6630 ft
RATE OF FIRE (cyclic) 480 rpm
RATE OF FIRE (practical) 220 rpm
M.V. (HE tracer) 900 m/s 2953 ft/sec
PROJECTILE WEIGHT (HE tracer) 0.119 kg
  0.2625 lb

1, 2. *2 cm Gebirgsflak 38*

7.5 cm GebirgsKanone M.11

In 1910 the German firm of Ehrhardt produced an export model in the shape of a 7.5 cm mountain gun. Only one country, Norway, bought any and a total of nine batteries were sent to Norway to equip their mountain batteries. These guns were known as the M.11, and could be broken down into six loads for transport. In 1940 many were still in use as improved ammunition had been developed for them, and many fell into German hands. They used some as the 7.5 cm GebK 247(n), despite their age, to equip occupation units. It is interesting to note that while German sources refer to this piece as a gun, all other sources refer to it as a howitzer.

DATA

CALIBRE 75 mm 2.95 in
LENGTH OF PIECE (L/17) 1275 mm
   50.2 in
WEIGHT IN ACTION 509 kg 1122 lb
ELEVATION −5° to 36°

TRAVERSE 6°
M.V. 315 m/s 1033 ft/sec
MAXIMUM RANGE 6900 m 7548 yards
SHELL WEIGHT 6.5 kg 14.33 lb

1, 2. *Norwegian M.11, the Ehrhardt 7.5 cm Gebirgskanone M.11*

2

7.5 cm leichte Infantriegeschutz 18. L/11.8

One of the most widely used guns in service with the Wehrmacht was the 7.5 cm le.IG 18. Development of this small gun was started by Rheinmetall in 1927 and it was issued to the support companies of infantry regiments and some mountain units. It had an unusual loading system in which the barrel was totally enclosed in a square slipper which pivoted upwards while the breech block remained fixed. Early guns had spoked wheels while later guns used pneumatic tyres. A special variant was the 7.5 cm le.IG 18F which was produced in 1939. This was a special para-drop variant with small wheels, no shield and the ability to be broken down into four 140 kg (308 lb) loads carried in containers. Only six were built. Another variant was the 7.5 cm le.GebIG 18.

DATA
CALIBRE 75 mm 2.95 in
LENGTH OF PIECE (L/11.8) 900 mm
  35.43 in
LENGTH OF BARREL 884 mm 34.8 in
LENGTH OF RIFLING 674 mm 26.5 in
WEIGHT IN ACTION 400 kg 882 lb
ELEVATION −10° to 73°
TRAVERSE 12°

M.V. (max with 13.2 lb shell) 210 m/s
  690 ft/sec
MAXIMUM RANGE 3550 m 3884 yards
SHELL WEIGHT (HE) 6 and 5.45 kg
  13.2 and 12 lb
SHELL WEIGHT (hollow charge) 3 kg
  6.6 lb

1

2

1, 2. *7.5 cm leIG 18*

7.5 cm leichte Gebirgs Infantriegeshutz 18. L/11.8

Intended as a temporary equipment until the later GebG 36 could enter service, the 7.5 cm le.GebIG 18 was very similar to the le.IG 18 and used the same barrel. It differed in having a tubular split trail and spoked wheels were standard. It could be broken down into six or ten loads for pack transport and the heaviest load weighed 74.9 kg (165 lb). The ability to be stripped for transport resulted in a heavier gun than the le.IG 18 but despite its temporary status it remained in service until 1945. It was issued at the rate of two guns to a mountain battalion.

DATA
As 7.5 cm le.IG 18 except:—
WEIGHT IN ACTION   440 kg   970 lb

7.5 cm leGebIG 18

7.5 cm Infantriegeschutz. L/13

DATA
CALIBRE 75 mm 2.95 in
LENGTH OF PIECE (L/13) 975 mm
  38.38 in
WEIGHT IN ACTION 375 kg 827 lb
ELEVATION −5° to 43°
TRAVERSE 50°
M.V. (max) 305 m/s 1000 ft/sec
MAXIMUM RANGE 5100 m 5580 yards
SHELL WEIGHT (HE) 4.5 or 6.35 kg
  10 or 14 lb

Only a few of the Rheinmetall guns known as the 7.5 cm Infantriegeschutz L/13 were produced, and no dates can be found regarding development and issue. The few built did see service. The L/13 was a development of the earlier le.IG 18 but had a conventional barrel, split telescopic trails and used different ammunition. For transport it could be broken down into four or six loads.

7.5 cm IG 37. L/22

DATA
CALIBRE 75 mm 2.95 in
LENGTH OF PIECE (L/22) 1815 mm
  71.45 in
LENGTH OF RIFLING 1340 mm 52.75 in
WEIGHT IN ACTION 510 kg 1124.5 lb
ELEVATION −10° to 40°
TRAVERSE 58°
M.V. (HE) 280 m/s 919 ft/sec
MAXIMUM RANGE 5150 m 5634 yards
SHELL WEIGHT (HE) 5.45 kg 12 lb

By 1944 production facilities in the remaining German territories were being stretched to such an extent that the output of infantry guns could not meet demand, and a hasty stop-gap measure was devised in the shape of the 7.5 cm IG 37. This gun was originally designated the 7.5 cm Pak 37 and was a captured Russian barrel cut down to L/22 and mounted on the carriage of the obsolete 3.7 cm Pak 35/36. A muzzle brake was fitted and the gun could fire a wide range of ammunition including a hollow-charge shell for use against AFVs. One oddity about this piece is that some barrels were mounted on the carriage of the 37 mm Model 1930 which was the Russian version of the 3.7 cm Pak 35/36. Many of these Russian guns had been captured in 1941-1942 and kept in store or in use as the 3.7 cm Pak 158(r), so the use of them for the 7.5 cm IG 37 was a cheap way of producing a much-needed infantry weapon from late 1944 until the end of the war.

7.5 cm Infantriegeschutz 42. L/22

The IG 42 was another 1944 improvisation produced in an attempt to provide enough infantry guns to meet demand. This time the barrel of the IG 37 was mounted on the carriage of the 8 cm PAW 600. These carriages had become available because of design and production difficulties experienced with the barrel of the PAW 600, a high-low pressure gun developed from the 8.1 cm Pak 8H63, and intended to be the standard German anti-tank gun. The new carriage was light and had many novel features, but not many IG 42s were issued. A smooth-bore version of this gun was under development as the war ended, along with fin-stabilised anti-tank projectiles.

DATA
As for 7.5 cm IG 37 except for:—
ELEVATION   −6° to 32°
TRAVERSE   60°
WEIGHT IN ACTION   590 kg   1300 lb

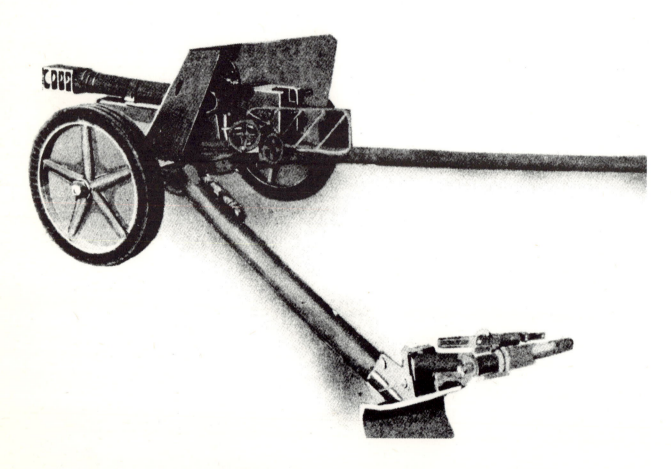

7.5 cm Gebirgsgeschutz 36. L/19.3

In 1935 Rheinmetall started to develop what was to become the standard gun of the mountain batteries, and in 1938 the result, known as the 7.5 cm GebG 36, entered service. The new gun had several novel features including a variable recoil facility and a large muzzle brake. It could be dismantled into eight loads but it was rather heavy for its role. However, it was popular with its crews for its stability when fired and its general ease of handling. Its replacement was intended to be a weapon using the design designation Gerät 99. Both Rheinmetall and Bohler submitted designs, but the choice was the Bohler entry which then became the 7.5 cm GebG 43. Only four had been completed by the time the war ended.

DATA

CALIBRE 75 mm 2.95 in	ELEVATION −10° to 70°
LENGTH OF PIECE (L/19.3) 1447.5 mm 56.98 in	TRAVERSE 40°
	M.V. 475 m/s 1558 ft/sec
LENGTH OF RIFLING 972 mm 38.27 in	MAXIMUM RANGE 9150 m 10010 yards
WEIGHT IN ACTION 750 kg 1654 lb	SHELL WEIGHT (HE) 5.83 kg 12.85 lb

1

1, 2, 3. *7.5 cm GebG 36*

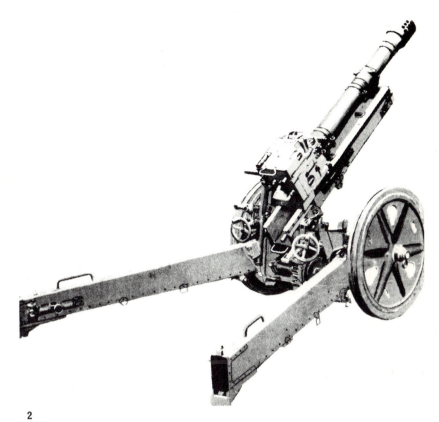

2

3

10.5 cm Gebirgshaubitze 40. L/30

The 10.5 cm GebH 40 entered service in 1936 after design and development by Bohler. It was an advanced and unusual design with a split trail carriage which caused the wheels to 'toe-in' when the trails were opened. The wheels could be removed for emplacement or for a special sledge to be fitted. It was intended that the gun would not normally be broken down into pack loads but into four sub-assemblies for towing by SdKfz 2 Kleines Kettenrad half-tracks. A version with a strengthened axle was intended for use with parachute troops. A range of special ammunition was designed for this piece.

DATA

CALIBRE	105 mm	4.13 in
LENGTH OF PIECE	3100 mm	122.05 in
LENGTH OF BARREL	2870 mm	112.94 in
LENGTH OF RIFLING	2407 mm	94.74 in
WEIGHT IN ACTION	1660 kg	3660 lb

ELEVATION	−5°30′ to 71°	
TRAVERSE	50°40′	
M.V.	570 m/s	1870 ft/sec
MAXIMUM RANGE	12625 m	13810 yards
SHELL WEIGHT (HE)	14.81 kg	32.65 lb

7.5 cm Leichtgeschutz 40. L/10

DATA
CALIBRE   75 mm   2.95 in
LENGTH OF PIECE   750 mm   29.5 in
LENGTH OF RIFLING   252 mm   9.92 in
WEIGHT IN ACTION   145 kg   321 lb
ELEVATION   −15° to 42°
TRAVERSE BELOW 20°   360°
TRAVERSE above 20°   60°
M.V.   350 m/s   1150 ft/sec
MAXIMUM RANGE   6800 m   7435 yards
SHELL WEIGHT (HE)   5.83 kg   12.85 lb

The first of the German recoilless guns to enter service was the LG 1, designed by Krupp and mounted on a light carriage with wire-spoked wheels. This gun was later mounted on a modified carriage with solid disc wheels and redesignated the 7.5 cm LG 40. It was used in action during the Crete landings in 1941 by the German Fallschirmjäger when it was dropped in four separate containers (later only two were used). The gun's construction was very light, and it featured a large breech block opening to the right. When emplaced the gun rested on a tripod made up of the three trail legs (the LG 1 had only two trails) and the barrel could be traversed 360°. As well as being used by paratroops the LG 40 was also issued to infantry and mountain units but it had tactical disadvantages and also required special safety precautions when fired.

1. 7.5 cm LG 40 **2.** *7.5 cm LG 1*

1

2

7.5 cm Ruckstossfreie Kanone 43

The 7.5 cm RfK 43 was a Krupp development to produce a simple and light recoil-less gun for infantry use. The barrel was placed on a small tripod on a circular base, with a swivel mounting using no elevation or traverse controls. For loading the entire breech block and venturi was removed using a bayonet lock. A plastic cartridge was inserted together with a hollow-charge shell and the breech replaced. The barrel was sighted with simple sights and fired by percussion. The RfK 43 was issued in small numbers but was not popular with its users. A similar weapon designed by Bohler did not see service.

7.5 cm RfK 43

DATA

CALIBRE 75 mm 2.95 in	MAXIMUM RANGE 2000 m 2180 yards	
WEIGHT IN ACTION 43.1 kg 95 lb	FIGHTING RANGE 300 m 327 yards	
TRAVERSE 360°	SHELL WEIGHT 4 kg 8.8 lb	
M.V. 170 m/s 556 ft/sec		

10.5 cm Leichtgeschutz 40. L/13

Introduced into service in 1943 the 10.5 cm LG 40 was a scaled-up 7.5 cm LG 40 barrel on a new carriage with a short box trail and an optional shield. It had the design designation LG 2(350)Kp, and apart from the carriage changes differed mainly in having the firing mechanism on top of the breech instead of the side. Designed primarily for use by paratroops, it could be dropped in four containers or complete in a specially designed tubular frame. On the ground it was towed by a SdKfz 2 Kleines Kettenrad, and this combination could be accommodated in a Gotha Go 242 glider. The LG 40/1 and 40/2 were minor variations of the basic LG 40.

10.5 cm LG 2(350)kp

10.5 cm LG 40 in action clearly showing the main disadvantages of a recoilless gun

DATA

CALIBRE 105 mm 4.13 in	TRAVERSE 80°
LENGTH OF PIECE (L/13) 1902 mm 74.88 in	M.V. (HE) 335 m/s 1099 ft/sec
LENGTH OF BARREL 1380 mm 54.33 in	M.V. (hollow-charge) 373 m/s 1224 ft/sec
LENGTH OF RIFLING 798 mm 31.4 in	MAXIMUM RANGE (HE) 7950 m 8694 yards
WEIGHT IN ACTION 388 kg 855.5 lb	SHELL WEIGHT (HE) 14.8 kg 32.6 lb
ELEVATION −15° to 40°30′	

10.5 cm Leichtgeschutz 42. L/17.5

The Rheinmetall-designed 10.5 cm LG 42 entered service in 1943. Its design designation was 10.5 cm LG 2 Rh and differed from the Krupp LG 40 mainly in carriage construction. Three trail legs could be folded out to form a tripod when in action and the two-wheeled towing axle was then off the ground. The carriage was constructed from tubular steel rather than the light alloys of earlier guns, and could be broken down into five loads. The LG 42/1 differed only in having a lighter and simpler tripod carriage.

DATA

CALIBRE   105 mm   4.13 in
LENGTH OF PIECE (L/17.5)   1836 mm   72.28 in
LENGTH OF BARREL   1374 mm   54.1 in
LENGTH OF RIFLING   798 mm   31.41 in
WEIGHT IN ACTION (LG 42)   552 kg   1217 lb

WEIGHT IN ACTION (LG 42/1)   540 kg   1191 lb
ELEVATION   15° to 42°35′
TRAVERSE BELOW 20°   360°
TRAVERSE ABOVE 20°   71°15′
M.V.   335 m/s   1099 ft/sec
MAXIMUM RANGE   7950 m   8694 yards
SHELL WEIGHT   14.8 kg   32.6 lb

10.5 cm LG 42
10.5 cm LG 42/1

10.5 cm Leichtgeschutz 43

This gun was essentially similar to the LG 42 and differed mainly in the carriage construction. It was designed as an infantry weapon and appears to have been produced in relatively small numbers. One item of interest about this gun is that it could be broken down into ten loads without the use of any tools other than the elevating and traversing handwheels.

DATA

CALIBRE   105 mm   4.13 in
LENGTH OF PIECE   1845 mm   72.66 in
LENGTH OF BARREL   1377 mm   54.26 in
LENGTH OF RIFLING   789 mm   31.06 in
WEIGHT COMPLETE   523.7 kg   1154.75 lb
ELEVATION   −25° to 40°

TRAVERSE AT 13°   360°
TRAVERSE AT 40°   70°
M.V.   335 m/s   1099 ft/sec
MAXIMUM RANGE   7950 m   8694 yards
SHELL WEIGHT   14.8 kg   32.6 lb

15 cm schwere Infantriegeschutz 33. L/11.4

Of all the German infantry guns produced the most powerful was the 15 cm s.IG 33. First produced by Rheinmetall in 1927, the s.IG 33 was a large heavy gun that looked clumsy and archaic, mainly because of its 1100 mm (43.3 in) diameter steel wheels, but the design was sound and robust so that the gun remained in service until 1945. Firing in both the upper and lower registers, the s.IG 33 fired either HE, smoke or hollow-charge shells, and a muzzle stick-bomb weighing 89.5 kg (197.3 lb) could be used to destroy wire entanglements and strong points up to a range of 1025 m (1120 yards). The main disadvantage of the s.IG 33 was its weight and prior to 1939 some attempts were made to use light alloys in the carriage construction. The result was not put into large-scale production due to the shortage of light alloys after 1939, so it was only when the s.IG 33 was put onto a mobile carriage that its full potential could be fully exploited. It was placed on a wide range of tracked vehicles and was ultimately developed into the 15 cm Sturmhaubitze 43, L/12.

DATA

CALIBRE   149.1 mm   5.87 in
LENGTH OF BARREL   1650 mm   64.9 in
LENGTH OF RIFLING   1346 mm   53 in
WEIGHT IN ACTION   1750 kg   3859 lb
ELEVATION   0° to 73°
TRAVERSE   11°30′
M.V.   240 m/s   790 ft/sec
MAXIMUM RANGE   4700 m   5140 yards
SHELL WEIGHT (HE)   38 kg   83.8 lb

SELF-PROPELLED CARRIAGES

15 cm sIG 33 auf GW 1 Ausf.B
15 cm sIG 33 auf Fgst PzKpfw 11(Sf) Verälngert
15 cm sIG 33 auf Fgst PzKpfw 11 (Sf) SdKfz 121
15 cm sIG 33(Sf) auf PzKpfw 38(t) Ausf.H, Bison
15 cm sIG 33/1 auf GW 38(t)
15 cm sIG 33 auf Pz 111

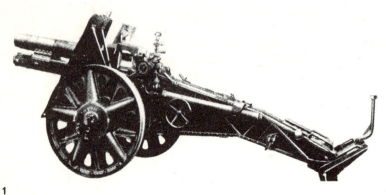

1

1, 4. *15 cm sIG 33* **2.** *15 cm sIG 33 with*
with muzzle stick bomb **3.** *15 cm sIG 33*
with rubber tyres for tractor towing by
Panzergrenadier units

2

3

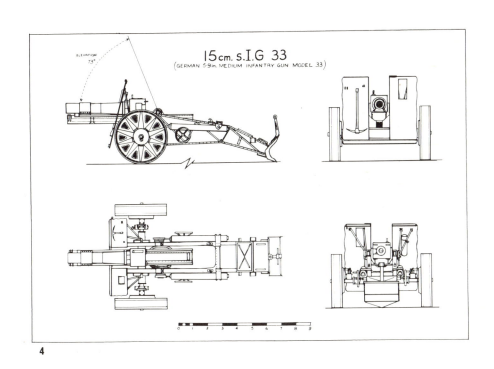

4

ITALY

Cannone da 47/32 modello 35

For the Italian Army the Böhler-designed Cannone da 47/32 modello 35 was a maid of all work. They used it as an infantry gun, as an anti-tank gun and it was also used as part of the equipment of the Italian Alpine divisions. For the alpine role the 47/32 could be broken down into five loads for carriage by mule but in infantry support units it could be towed by either a light truck or horses. By 1943 it had almost relinquished the anti-tank role and was used increasingly as an infantry support weapon. During the North African campaigns large numbers of these guns were captured by Allied forces and after refurbishing at the Captured Stores Depot at Alexandria, one hundred were reissued for use by Allied units. A further 96 were modified for dropping by parachute and were also issued to Allied troops. These latter guns were also modified to enable the layer to fire the gun, whereas the normal method was that another crew member did the actual firing. A No 22 sighting telescope was fitted and a 6 pr shoulder pad was added to assist the layer.

DATA

CALIBRE 47 mm 1.85 in
LENGTH OF PIECE (L/35.8) 1680 mm 66.2 in
LENGTH OF RIFLING 1328 mm 52.3 in
WEIGHT IN ACTION 277 kg 610.8 lb
ELEVATION −10° to 56°
TRAVERSE 60°
M.V. (HE) 250 m/s 820 ft/sec

MAXIMUM RANGE 4300 m 4704 yards
SHELL WEIGHT 2.37 kg 5.2 lb

SELF-PROPELLED CARRIAGES

Carro Commando Compagnia Semoventi da 47/32—PanzerBefehlwagen 47/32 (770)(i)

Cannone da 65/17

The Cannone da 65/17 was first produced in 1913 at the Turin Arsenal and it entered service soon afterwards with the Italian Alpine divisions. By 1940 there were still over 700 in service but many had been withdrawn from the Alpine units and were in use as infantry support guns. The 65/17 was meant to have an anti-tank role but the rounds issued were ineffective and remained little used. There was little of note about the design—it did not normally have a shield and could be broken down into six loads. Some passed into German service as the 6.5 cm GebK 246(i) but the numbers involved appear to have been small.

DATA

CALIBRE 65 mm 2.56 in	ELEVATION −7°30′ to 20°
LENGTH OF PIECE (L/17.7) 1150 mm 45.275 in	TRAVERSE 8°
	M.V. 348 m/s 1142 ft/sec
LENGTH OF RIFLING (L/13.9) 905 mm 35.63 in	MAXIMUM RANGE 6500 m 7111 yards
WEIGHT IN ACTION 556 kg 1226 lb	SHELL WEIGHT (HE) 4.24 kg 9.35 lb

Cannone da 70/15

One of the most elderly designs used during World War Two was the Italian Cannone da 70/15. Its basic design was already rather ancient when the first gun was built at the Turin Arsenal in 1902 and the first guns were issued to Italian mountain units in 1904. It was replaced in mountain use by the Cannone da 65/17 and the 70/15 was passed over to the infantry for use as an infantry support gun. By 1941 the 70/15 was obsolete but it remained in use in Africa and especially in Eritrea and Ethiopia where it was encountered by the Allied forces in the short campaigns during 1941 and 1942. The 70/15 could be broken down into four loads, and was probably the only weapon of its type in use during 1939-1945 that did not employ any form of recoil mechanism. All recoil forces were absorbed by a trail spade and a rope arrangement attached to the axle.

DATA

CALIBRE 70 mm 2.756 in
LENGTH OF PIECE (L/16.4) 1150 mm
  45.275 in
LENGTH OF RIFLING (L/13.5) 944 mm
  37.165 in
WEIGHT IN ACTION 387 kg 853.33 lb

ELEVATION −12° to 21°
TRAVERSE 0°
M.V. 353 m/s 1158 ft/sec
MAXIMUM RANGE 6630 m 7253 yards
SHELL WEIGHT 4.84 kg 10.67 lb

Obice da 75/18 M34

The Obice da 75/18 was an Ansaldo howitzer produced in 1934 to replace the existing mountain guns in service with the Italian Army. It used the same barrel as the Obice da 75/18 M35, a field howitzer, on a special mountain carriage designed to break down into eight loads. The design was modern and had a good performance, so that after 1943 the Germans were glad to be able to take over as many as they could as the 7.5 cm GebH 254(i).

DATA

CALIBRE	75 mm 2.95 in	WEIGHT TRAVELLING	820 kg 1808 lb
LENGTH OF PIECE (L/20.75)	1557 mm 61.3 in	WEIGHT IN ACTION	780 kg 1720 lb
LENGTH OF BARREL (L/18.27)	1370 mm 53.93 in	ELEVATION	−10° to 65°
LENGTH OF RIFLING (L/15.1)	1133.5 mm 44.626 in	TRAVERSE	48°
		M.V. (max)	428 m/s 1404 ft/sec
		MAXIMUM RANGE	9560 m 10458 yards
		SHELL WEIGHT	6.3 kg 13.89 lb

JAPAN

37 mm Infantry Gun Type 11

The Type 11 infantry gun entered service in 1922 and remained in production until 1937. It was the Japanese version of the French Canon d'Infantrie de 37 mle 1916, but the Japanese copy varied in some details. The Japanese gun was lighter due to the use of tubular steel in the tripod and the Type 11 was intended to be carried into action and thus had no wheels. In typical Japanese fashion, the Type 11 was carried on poles by four men. The usual round fired was HE but a rather optimistic anti-tank round was provided. By 1941 the Type 11 was obsolete but remained in service simply because there was not another gun to replace it. Full Japanese designation of the Type 11 was Juichinen Shiki Heisha Hoheiho.

DATA

CALIBRE 37 mm 1.456 in	TRAVERSE 33°	
LENGTH OF PIECE (L/22) 927 mm 36.5 in	M.V. 451 m/s 1480 ft/sec	
LENGTH OF BARREL 813 mm 32 in	MAXIMUM RANGE (approx) 2400 m 2625 yards	
LENGTH EMPLACED 2103 mm 82.8 in		
WEIGHT IN ACTION 93.4 kg 205.75 lb	SHELL WEIGHT (HE) 0.645 kg 1.42 lb	
ELEVATION −4.8° to 14°		

37 mm Gun Type 94

The 37 mm Gun Type 94 entered service in 1934 and was intended for use as an anti-tank and close support gun for infantry. By 1941 its anti-tank performance was insufficient against modern tanks and the gun was used as an infantry support weapon. For this role it fired HE and shrapnel rounds. Like most Japanese guns the Type 94 was light and unremarkable in design. It remained in use until 1945. Full Japanese designation was Kyuyon Shiki Sanjunana Miri Ho, but only the last three words were commonly used.

DATA

CALIBRE	37 mm 1.456 in		TRAVERSE	60°
LENGTH OF BARREL (L/45.6)	1686.5 mm 66.4 in		M.V. (max)	700 m/s 2300 ft/sec
WEIGHT IN ACTION	321.3 kg 714 lb		MAXIMUM RANGE	4570 m 5000 yards
ELEVATION	−10° to 27°		SHELL WEIGHT (HE)	0.486 kg 1.07 lb

70 mm Battalion Gun Type 92

Despite its odd appearance the little Type 92 battalion gun was one of the most successful infantry support weapons used by any of the combatants during World War Two. It was small, light and handy and could fire a useful round, but probably its best attribute as far as the Japanese were concerned was that it was available in some numbers. In action the Type 92 was used right up with the forward troops and was able to fire direct over open sights. In the jungle it was used to provide a steady harassing fire—a few rounds would be fired from one position and the gun would then be swiftly and easily taken to another location to fire another few rounds. The lightness and ease of handling was one of the Type 92s biggest advantages but the official number of men required to manhandle it was ten although only five were used in action and the gun was frequently towed by horses or mules. First issued in 1932 the Type 92 remained in use until 1945. It could fire HE, smoke and shrapnel and a rather ineffective AP round was available. A basic propellant charge with three increments could provide a wide range variation with a minimum range of as little as 110 yards (100 m). Full Japanese designation was Kyuni Shiki Hoheiho.

DATA

CALIBRE   70 mm   2.756 in
LENGTH OF BARREL   622 mm   24.5 in
LENGTH EMPLACED   2006 mm   79 in
HEIGHT EMPLACED   775 mm   30.5 in
WIDTH OVERALL   914 mm   36 in
WEIGHT IN ACTION   212.47 kg   468 lb
ELEVATION   −10° to 50°
TRAVERSE   90°
M.V.   198 m/s   650 ft/sec
MAXIMUM EFFECTIVE RANGE   1373 m   1500 yards
MAXIMUM RANGE (approx)   2745 m   3000 yards
SHELL WEIGHT (HE)   3.795 kg   8.36 lb

DATA
CALIBRE 75 mm 2.95 in
LENGTH OF PIECE (L/19.2) 1440 mm
 56.7 in
LENGTH OF BARREL 1105 mm 43.5 in
LENGTH EMPLACED 4318 mm 170 in
WIDTH 1219 mm 48 in
WEIGHT IN ACTION 544 kg 1199.5 lb
ELEVATION −18° to 40°
TRAVERSE 6°
M.V. 435 m/s 1427 ft/sec
MAXIMUM RANGE 7022 m 7675 yards
SHELL WEIGHT (HE Type 94) 6.02 kg
 13.27 lb

75 mm Regimental Gun Type 41

The first Type 41 pack guns were built at Osaka Arsenal in 1908 and were originally licence-built versions of the Krupp M.08 mountain gun. It was not long before the Japanese modified the carriage to reduce weight and the gun remained in service for many years until it was replaced by the Type 94 after 1934. After 1934 the Type 41 was used as an infantry support weapon and redesignated as a regimental gun. It remained in use until 1945 and is still in Chinese service in 1974. For pack transport the Type 41 dismantled into six parts but it was normally horse-towed. Full Japanese designation was Yonichi Shiki Sampo.

75 mm Mountain (Pack) Gun Type 94

The design of the Type 94 was based on that of the Type 41 and replaced it in service with the Japanese mountain artillery regiments. Compared with the older gun the Type 94, which entered service in 1934, had a revised trail, a longer barrel and a sliding breech block. The overall design was modern and sturdy and the gun could be broken down into eleven loads for carrying on six animals. Assembly took about ten minutes and the gun could be broken down in three-five minutes. If necessary the gun could be carried by eighteen men but over difficult country more men would be needed. The Type 94 remained in Japanese service until 1945 and in 1974 still remains in use with the North Vietnamese. Although intended for use with the Japanese paratroop arm, the Type 94 does not appear to have seen action in that role.

DATA

CALIBRE 75 mm 2.95 in
LENGTH OF BARREL (L/20.8) 1562 mm 61.5 in
LENGTH OF RIFLING 997 mm 39.25 in
LENGTH TRAILS OPEN 3810 mm 150 in
HEIGHT 889 mm 35 in
TRACK WIDTH 1016 mm 40 in

WEIGHT IN ACTION 536.3 kg 1181.3 lb
ELEVATION —10° to 45°
TRAVERSE 40°
M.V. (max) 355 m/s 1165 ft/sec
MAXIMUM RANGE 8178 m 8938 yards
SHELL WEIGHT (Type 97 HE) 6.18 kg 13.62 lb

NORWAY

7.5 cm M.27 (Kongsberg)

To supplement the Erhardt 75 mm guns already in service with the Norwegian mountain batteries, in 1927 the Norwegian firm of Kongsberg Kanonfabrik produced a 7.5 cm mountain gun known as the M.27. Only twenty-four guns were made and all were still in service in 1939. There are no records of the Germans using any after their invasion in 1940.

DATA

CALIBRE 75 mm 2.95 in	TRAVERSE 5°	
LENGTH OF BARREL (L/20.5) 1537 mm 60.53 in	M.V. 395 m/s 1296 ft/sec	
WEIGHT IN ACTION 600 kg 1323 lb	MAXIMUM RANGE 8800 m 9627 yards	
ELEVATION −5° to 47°	SHELL WEIGHT 6.5 kg 14.33 lb	

SWEDEN

Bofors 75 mm Model 1934

The Bofors Model 1934 Mountain Howitzer was one of the Swedish company's more successful products between the wars for it was sold to a large number of countries. It was a development of the earlier Model 1928, an L/20 piece, and could be broken down into a variety of loads for towing by mules or tractors. When towed in one load the end of the box trail was raised up over the centre portion to ease handling. As well as equipping the Swedish mountain artillery units the Model 1934 was also bought by Germany to add a degree of modern equipment to the ageing artillery park of the Gebirgstruppe. The German designation was 7.5 cm GebH 34. China also bought a batch as did many South American states, including Argentina. A later model, the Model 1936, was bought by Bulgaria.

DATA

CALIBRE 75 mm 2.95 in	TRAVERSE 6°	
LENGTH OF BARREL (L/22) 1650 mm 65 in	M.V. 470 m/s 1542 ft/sec	
WEIGHT IN ACTION 790 kg 1742 lb	MAXIMUM RANGE 10000 m 10940 yards	
ELEVATION — 10° to 50°	SHELL WEIGHT (HE) 6.5 kg 14.33 lb	

UNITED KINGDOM

Ordnance, Q.F., 6-pr. Mark 2 on Carriage Mark 3

When the future equipment of the British airborne forces was considered in late 1942 it was decided that glider-borne troops would carry some form of anti-tank gun. The 6 pr was decided upon but in its standard form it was too wide for the 4 foot 6 inch width of the Horsa glider fuselage. A small batch of 6 pr carriages were therefore modified to become the Carriage Mark 3, with the main change being made to the axletree which was shortened. Other changes were the removal of the fixed frontal armour and slight changes to the shield. The elevating handwheel was moved to above the sights and angled to the left. The trail legs were made in two halves joined at the centre by a socket joint to reduce the length, and the usual trail eye was replaced by an L-shaped bracket. Once on the ground the gun was towed by a modified jeep. In action the gun was provided with HE as well as AP ammunition and by 1945 APDS shot was issued which enabled the gun to penetrate 146 mm of armour at 1000 yards. The airborne 6 pr was used in action at Arnhem in September 1944 when a total of 26 were landed, and the type was also used during and after the Rhine Crossings in March 1945. As a possible alternative to glider delivery, experiments were made to drop a 6 pr and jeep from a Halifax Mark 1X. Four 60 foot parachutes were used and the results were successful but the method does not appear to have been used in action.

1. *In this view of a Mark 3 carriage trail can be seen the joint bolts. Behind is a 3.7 inch howitzer packed for loading into a glider.* **2.** *Airborne 6 pr in action* **3.** *Ordnance, Q.F., 6 pr Mark 2 on Carriage Mark 3*

1

2

3

Q.F. 3.7-inch, Howitzer, Mark 1, on Carriage, 3.7-inch 3.7-inch Howr., Mark 1VP

The design of a new mountain howitzer to replace existing guns in British service was started in 1915 and the first guns were issued in February 1917. It was the first British gun to feature a split trail, but retained the 'screw barrel' feature inherited from earlier guns. The large shield was intended for use on the Indian frontier and was often removed for service elsewhere. Most of the guns produced were used in India and many others were issued to various colonial forces. A detachment of nine men was needed to serve the gun which broke down into loads for five mules with other mules for carrying the ammunition. After World War One consideration was given to using the 3.7-inch 'Pack Howitzer' (as it was generally known) as an infantry support weapon. The spoked wheels were replaced by pneumatic tyres and a No. 23 trailer was added to enable the gun to be towed by a motor vehicle. During 1932 a decision was made that the 3-inch mortar would serve as the infantry support weapon and after that the 3.7-inch howitzer faded from the infantry gun scene. However, in 1939 many were still in service and many saw action in the Far East, especially in Burma. They served well throughout the war and were still in use in 1945. During the early days of the British Airborne Forces the 3.7-inch howitzer was the standard artillery piece but it was soon replaced by more modern equipment. Any of these guns that were captured by the Germans were used by them as the 9.4 cm GebH 301(e) until all captured ammunition had been expended.

DATA
CALIBRE 94 mm 3.7 in
LENGTH OF PIECE (L/12.65) 1189 mm 46.8 in
LENGTH OF BORE (L/11.83) 1112 mm 43.8 in
LENGTH OF RIFLING 906.4 mm 35.685 in
WEIGHT TRAVELLING (with trailer) 2218.2 kg 4886 lb
WEIGHT TRAVELLING (w/o trailer) 773.3 kg 1705 lb
WEIGHT IN ACTION 757 kg 1669 lb
ELEVATION −5° to 40°
TRAVERSE 40°
M.V. (max, Charge 5) 296.7 m/s 973 ft/sec
MAXIMUM RANGE 5490 m 6000 yards
SHELL WEIGHT (HE) 9.08 kg 20 lb

1. *Q.F. 3.7-inch, Howitzer, Mark 1*
2, 3. *Indian mountain batteries in Burma with 3.7-inch howitzers*

1

2

3

4. *3.7-inch Pack Howitzer in Burma, February 1944* **5.** *British mountain battery training in Wales with a Pack Howitzer*

4

5

Platform, 40 mm A.A. Mountings, Mark 4

The Platform Mark 4 was an adaptation of the basic Bofors Mark 3 Platform which could be used to enable a Bofors 40 mm anti-aircraft gun to be stowed within the close confines of a glider or transport aircraft fuselage. On the Mark 4 platform the outrigger arms and the carriage wheels and axles could be removed from the platform and the platform then rested on four small castor wheels which enabled the gun and platform to be wheeled about in small spaces. The Mark 4 platform could accommodate the Bofors mountings Marks 1 to 4.

Ordnance, Q.F., 40 mm, on Mountings, 40 mm, A.A., Marks 9 and 10

The Bofors Mountings Marks 9 and 10 were the Mountings Marks 3 and 4 converted for mounting onto the Platform, 2-wheeled, 40 mm A.A., Mark 1. This platform was the result of a combination of Canadian and British designs intended to provide the 40 mm Bofors gun with a light platform suitable for jungle and airborne warfare. The result was a small two-wheeled platform which could be converted into a three-outrigger stand for firing. A great deal of detailed attention was given to keeping down the weight of the platform while at the same time ease of assembly and handling was given a great deal of consideration. Originally the Bofors Mark 1/2 gun was intended for use with this equipment but as development of this variant with its distinctive muzzle brake was not completed, it was replaced by the Mark 1 or 1*. For pack transport the entire platform, mounting and gun could be broken down into nine loads.

1, 2, 3. 40 mm Mark 1/2 on Mounting Marks 9 or 10 with Platform Two-wheeled Mark 1

1

2

3

Smooth Bore 3-inch, Mark 1, on Carriage, 3-inch, Mark 1

The Smith Gun was one of the several different forms of 'pipe gun' produced in the United Kingdom in 1940 to quickly replace the large numbers of conventional guns left behind at Dunkirk. It was a simple smooth-bore gun which ran on two 48-inch diameter (1219 mm) metal-disc wheels, and the entire gun was made from sheet steel with many nut-and-bolt joints where weldings would have been normal. In action, the gun was unusual in that it was designed to be turned onto the right hand wheel which then gave 360° traverse with the added advantage that the left-hand wheel gave the four man crew some measure of overhead protection. This protection was very necessary as the range of the gun was only about 500 yards and only 200 yards when firing the anti-tank round. Firing controls were almost non-existent but the Smith Gun was intended for indirect fire at targets up to 650 yards away. Rounds were fired by percussion after the round had been placed in the simple breech, and the propellant was in a cartridge secured to the base of the projectile. Up to ten rounds could be carried on the gun and a further forty could be carried in a trailer which was intended to be placed close to the gun in action. The Smith Gun was issued to Home Guard units and at one time it was intended to issue it to regular Home Defence units, but this does not appear to have happened. At least one Smith Gun was fitted to a Bren Gun Carrier for use by a Home Guard unit.

1

2

3

Mortar, Spigot, 29 mm, Mark 1

DATA
SPIGOT DIAMETER 29 mm 1.14 in
SPIGOT LENGTH 177.5 mm 6.99 in
WEIGHT IN ACTION 156.5 kg 345 lb
ELEVATION (MAX) approx 45°
TRAVERSE 360°
MAXIMUM RANGE 822 m 900 yards
BOMB WEIGHT 9.07 kg 20 lb
RATE OF FIRE 12 rpm

Among the many odd weapons turned out for Home Guard use in the desperate days of 1940 and 1941 was the Blacker Bombard. The designer, a Lt.Col. Blacker, was a proponent of the spigot mortar mainly because the barrel of the normal mortar could be replaced by a simple spigot rod over which a bomb of virtually any diameter could be placed and then fired. The Blacker Bombard followed this idea and was used by the Home Guard in some numbers. It was simple to produce and operate and it was also cheap. The propellant was black powder, and any recoil forces produced on firing were absorbed by the simple tubular steel quadrupod mount. Range was very limited and aiming was a matter of luck but the projectile carried a useful warhead. By some quirk of Army supply some of these bombards turned up in North Africa during the Siege of Tobruk and were used by some Indian Army units with varying degrees of success.

USA

75 mm Pack Howitzer M1A1 on Carriage M1

Development of the gun that was to become the 75 mm M1A1 began in 1920, and the design was standardised as the M1 in 1927. Some slight changes were made to produce the M1A1, these changes being made to the breech ring and block. The barrel was placed on the Carriage M1 which was designed for mountain warfare and could be broken down into six loads. The design was sturdy and modern and had an unusual feature in that the traverse handwheel operated directly on the axle. Thus the cradle incorporated only the elevation mechanism. At first production was slow for in June 1940 only 91 were in use. By December 1941 this had risen to 458. and by the time the war ended 4939 had been made. The M1A1 was used widely and many were issued to Allied forces, especially China.

DATA
CALIBRE   75 mm   2.95 in
LENGTH OVERALL   1321 mm   52 in
LENGTH OF BARREL (L/15.93)   1194.75 mm   47 in
WEIGHT COMPLETE   588.38 kg   1296 lb
ELEVATION   −5° to 45°
TRAVERSE   6°
M.V. (max)   381 m/s   1250 ft/sec
MAXIMUM RANGE (Shell M41A1)   8930 m   9760 yards
SHELL WEIGHT (Shell M41A1)   6.247 kg   13.76 lb.

1

2

1, 2, *75 mm Pack Howitzer M1A1*
3. *Jugoslav partisans being trained in the use of the 75 mm Pack Howitzer in 1944, Training was given by British Officers.*

75 mm Pack Howitzer in use with the Chinese Army

3

75 mm Pack Howitzer M1A1 on Carriage M8

Although the Carriage M1 was widely used with the 75 mm M1A1 it was gradually replaced by a carriage with rubber tyres which could be easily adapted for dropping by parachute. The basic carriage remained little changed but weight increased to 1340 lb—otherwise the same data applies as to the version with the M1 carriage. This new carriage was the Carriage M8, sometimes referred to as the Carriage (Airborne) M8. It gradually replaced the earlier version in service and it was also issued to many Allied forces. Some were issued to the British Airborne artillery units and various amphibious forces where it was known as the 75 mm Pack Howitzer Mark 1. For parachute delivery the equipment could be broken down into nine loads.

British 75 mm Pack Howitzer lashed in a Hamilcar glider

US Marines in action on Peleliu with a Pack Howitzer.   October 1944

Airborne 75 mm Pack Howitzer troops in training, December 1943

105 mm Howitzer M3—Carriage M3A1

The 105 mm Howitzer M3 was originally a shortened version of the 105 mm M2 field howitzer which was given the trial designation of T7. Its carriage was originally the T6 and it was designed from the start to be an airborne and jungle weapon. By the time the war ended 2580 had been produced and they served in all theatres. The most unusual feature of the howitzer and its carriage was that the axles could be turned through 180° to lower the piece onto a firing pedestal to give stability when firing. The recoil mechanism was a modification of that used on the 75 mm Field Howitzer M1A1, and a split trail was used. The weapon entered service during 1943 and served only with American units.

DATA

CALIBRE 105 mm 4.134 in
LENGTH OF BARREL (L/16) 1680 mm 66 in
WEIGHT 1132.7 kg 2495 lb
LENGTH TRAVELLING 3937 mm 155 in
HEIGHT 1117 mm 44 in
WIDTH 1710 mm 67.3125 in
TRACK 1440 mm 56.69 in
ELEVATION −9° to 30°
TRAVERSE 45°
M.V. 311 m/s 1020 ft/sec
MAXIMUM RANGE 6633 m 7250 yards
SHELL WEIGHT (HE,M1) 14.98 kg 33 lb

1, 2. *105 mm Howitzer M3—Carriage M3A1* **3.** *105 mm Howitzer M3 firing on Brest, 1944*

1

2

3

40 mm Gun Carriage M5 (Airborne)

The Gun Carriage M5 was developed for use with the 40 mm Automatic Antiaircraft Gun M1 which was the American version of the Bofors. It was designed so that the 40 mm Bofors could be carried in a C46, C46A, C47 or C54 transport aircraft and was so arranged that the gun and two of the carriage outriggers were carried separately from the remainder of the carriage on a small two-wheeled trailer. When in position the gun was mounted on a cruciform platform made of four steel beams, and the rest of the carriage was little different from the normal M2A1 carriage. Assembling the carriage took three men about five minutes and the gun could be prepared to travel in about eight minutes. The M5 was not used much for airborne work and was mainly used for jungle warfare.

DATA

OVERALL LENGTH TRAVELLING   2991 mm   117.75 in

LENGTH IN POSITION   4940 mm   194.5 in

WIDTH TRAVELLING   1422 mm   56 in

WIDTH IN POSITION   1746 mm   68.75 in

HEIGHT TRAVELLING   1924 mm   75.75 in

HEIGHT IN POSITION   1924 mm   75.75 in

WEIGHT TRAVELLING (with gun)   1580 kg   3480 lb

WEIGHT TRAVELLING (without gun)   1532 kg   3375 lb

WEIGHT IN ACTION   2040 kg   4495 lb

ELEVATION   −5° to 90°

TRAVERSE   360°

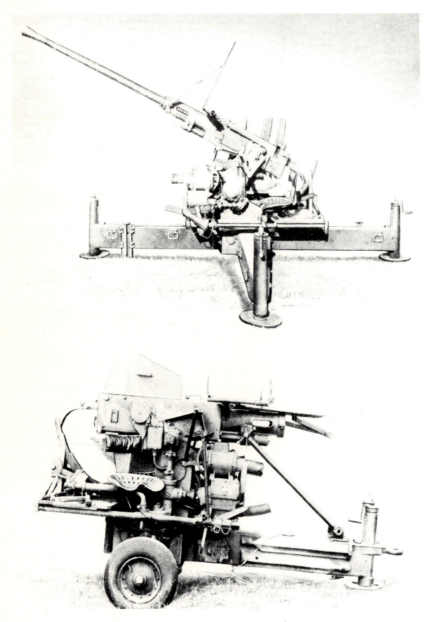

57 mm Recoilless Rifle M18

The first American recoilless rifle was built in 1943 as the T15 and was developed into the T15E1 ready for production as the M18. It can be regarded as the first piece of artillery that could be carried by one man to see service, and it could be fired from the shoulder but the normal method was to fire it from a tripod. The tripod most often used was modified from the M1917A2 Browning machine gun tripod. Only direct fire was possible with the M18 and it could fire HE, HEAT and canister rounds. All the rounds used were pre-rifled. The M18 entered service in late 1944 and was used mainly in the Pacific theatre.

DATA

CALIBRE	57 mm	2.244 in	ELEVATION ON TRIPOD		−27° to 65°
LENGTH OVERALL	1524 mm	60 in	TRAVERSE	360°	
LENGTH OF RIFLING	1179 mm	46.44 in	M.V.	372 m/s	1220 ft/sec
WEIGHT OF GUN	18.33 kg	40.375 lb	RANGE	4026 m	4400 yards

75 mm Recoilless Rifle M20

The success of the 57 mm M18 prompted the development of the recoilless principle in a heavier calibre, and in September 1944 the first 75 mm version was produced as the T25. This went into production as the M20 in March 1945 and the first guns issued were used in the Pacific theatre. It used the same M1917A1 machine gun tripod as the M18 but it could also be used for indirect fire. Like the 57 mm gun the M20 produced considerable back-blast which required special safety precautions when firing.

DATA

CALIBRE 75 mm 2.95 in
LENGTH OVERALL 2073 mm 81.6 in
LENGTH OF RIFLING 1646 mm 64.8 in
WEIGHT OF GUN 46.76 kg 103 lb

ELEVATION ON TRIPOD −27° to 65°
TRAVERSE 360°
M.V. 305 m/s 1000 ft/sec
RANGE 6405 m 7000 yards

1. *M20 in action on Okinawa, August, 1945*
2, 3. *75 mm Recoilless Rifle M20*

1

2

3

USSR

37 mm Infantry Gun Model 15R

The little Model 15R was a World War One veteran that had never passed out of Russian service and was still in limited service in 1941. It was a very simple rugged design that must have seemed rather archaic when it was first introduced in 1915.

DATA

CALIBRE 37 mm 1.456 in
LENGTH OF PIECE (L/19) 703 mm 27.68 in
WEIGHT IN ACTION 180 kg 397 lb
ELEVATION −5° to 15°

M.V. 442 m/s 1450 ft/sec
MAXIMUM RANGE 3200 m 3500 yards
SHELL WEIGHT 0.512 kg 1.129 lb

45 mm Infantry Howitzer Model 29K

Virtually no information has survived relating to the Model 29K infantry howitzer. It passed into German hands in small numbers in 1941 as the 4.5 cm IH 186(r) but what use they made of them is unknown.

DATA

CALIBRE 45 mm 1.77 in
LENGTH OF PIECE (L/25) 1125 mm 44.3 in
WEIGHT IN ACTION 240 kg 529 lb
ELEVATION −5° to 25°

TRAVERSE 90°
M.V. 600 m/s 1968 ft/sec
MAXIMUM RANGE 6000 m 6564 yards
SHELL WEIGHT 1.15 kg 2.536 lb

76.2 mm Infantry Gun Model 10P

Despite its age the Model 10P was still in Russian service in 1941. It entered service in 1910 and was built at the Putilov works. The design was unremarkable but like most Russian guns it was rugged and serviceable. After 1941 the type was used by the Germans as the 7.62 cm IG 289(r), mainly by second-line units. The gun was normally towed by four horses.

DATA

CALIBRE 76.2 mm 3 in
LENGTH OF PIECE (L/16.5) 1257 mm
  50 in
WEIGHT TRAVELLING 1156 kg 2549 lb
WEIGHT IN ACTION 570 kg 1257 lb

ELEVATION −12° to 18°
TRAVERSE 9½°
M.V. 275 m/s 902 ft/sec
MAXIMUM RANGE 2560 m 2800 yards
SHELL WEIGHT 6.55 kg 14.44 lb

1

2

76.2 mm Infantry Gun Model 1927 (76-27)

The Model 1927 infantry gun was one of the more successful Russian gun designs and was in widespread use with their forces as it was intended that it would replace all other infantry guns in use by them. Its design was basic and simple but sound—for instance the interrupted screw threads of the breech block engaged directly into the barrel as there was no breech ring. The wheels were 45 inches in diameter (1143 mm) and provided extra protection for the crew. After 1941 large numbers fell into German hands, and the Germans used them in some numbers. They went to the extent of making their own ammunition for them and even fitted them with German sights. Full German designation was 7.62 cm Infantriekanonehaubitze 290(r) or IKH 290(r), and the Germans used them on all fronts. The data below is extracted from an Allied intelligence report on guns captured in Normandy during July 1944.

DATA

CALIBRE	76.2 mm 3 in		WHEEL TRACK	1397 mm 55 in
LENGTH OF PIECE (L/16.5)	1257 mm 49.5 in		WEIGHT IN ACTION	780 kg 1720 lb
LENGTH OF BORE	1168 mm 46 in		ELEVATION	−6° to 25°
LENGTH OF RIFLING	777 mm 30.6 in		TRAVERSE	6°
LENGTH OVERALL	3556 mm 140 in		M.V. (HE)	387 m/s 1270 ft/sec
OVERALL HEIGHT	1321 mm 52 in		MAXIMUM RANGE	8555 m 9350 yards
OVERALL WIDTH	1689 mm 66.5 in		SHELL WEIGHT (HE)	6.21 kg 13.69 lb

1

2

76.2 mm Infantry Gun Model 1943 (76-43)

During 1943 the Russians introduced a revised version of the successful 76-27 which used a modified 76.2 mm infantry gun barrel on the carriage of the 45 mm anti-tank gun. The result was the 76.2 mm Model 1943 and was often referred to as a regimental gun. Using the 45 mm Model 1943 carriage meant that the Model 1943 was lighter than the Model 1927 gun and the new carriage also gave a greater degree of traverse which was useful for anti-tank work using hollow-charge projectiles.

DATA

CALIBRE 76.2 mm 3 in
LENGTH OF PIECE (L/16.5) 1257 mm
  49.5 in
LENGTH OF BORE 1168 mm 46 in
LENGTH OF RIFLING 777 mm 30.6 in
WEIGHT IN ACTION 600 kg 1323 lb

ELEVATION −8° to 25°
TRAVERSE 60°
M.V. 387 m/s 1270 ft/sec
MAXIMUM RANGE 8555 m 9350 yards
SHELL WEIGHT (HE) 6.21 kg 13.69 lb

Ampulenjot 1941 System Kartukow

DATA

CALIBRE 127 mm 5 in
BARREL LENGTH 1020 mm 40.16 in
BORE LENGTH 845 mm 33.3 in
WEIGHT 26 kg 57.3 lb
ELEVATION 0° to 12°
TRAVERSE 360°
M.V. 50 m/s 164 ft/sec
MAXIMUM RANGE 250 m 274 yards
PROJECTILE WEIGHT 1.5/1.8 kg 3.3/
  3.97 lb

One of the more unusual Russian light guns was the weapon emplaced in static positions to fire incendiary projectiles. In design it resembled the British 'pipe' guns such as the Northover Projector since it was a simple tube closed at the breech and using a black powder charge. There were no traversing or elevation controls apart from two handles. Exactly what status this weapon had is now difficult to determine but it has all the hallmarks of a hastily-produced home defence weapon.

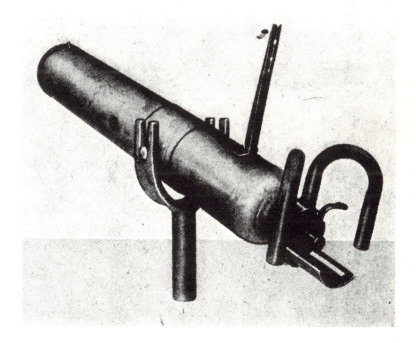

76.2 mm Recoilless Gun

The only record of a Russian recoilless gun that was used during World War Two comes from a German intelligence report dated June 1941. There is no mention of a Russian designation but it would appear that it was used as a static fortress gun mounted on a pedestal. At the breech end the presence of a venturi would indicate the use of conventional recoilless ammunition so it would appear that the Russians were well advanced in research on the subject. The reported range given below appears optimistic.

DATA

CALIBRE 76.2 mm 3 in		TRAVERSE 360°
LENGTH INCLUDING VENTURI 2230 mm 87.8 in		M.V. 360 m/s 1180 ft/sec
		MAXIMUM RANGE 7000 m 7658 yards
WEIGHT 200 kg 440 lb		PROJECTILE WEIGHT 4.7 kg 10.36 lb
ELEVATION −5° to 29°		

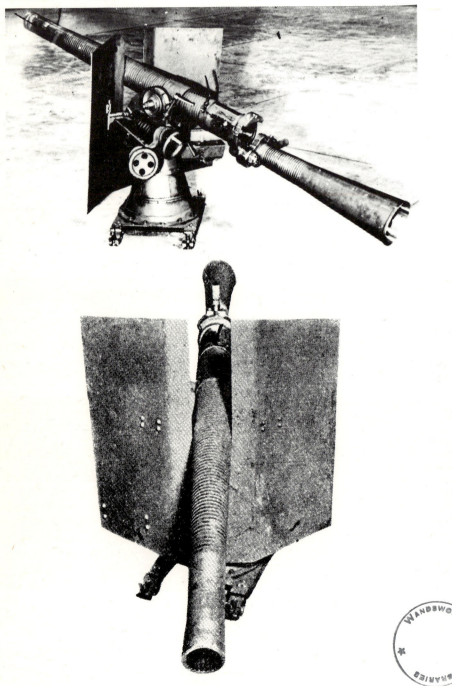